Karma

and

Frequency

By Tina Erwin

Karma and Frequency
Copyright © 2015 Tina Erwin
Published 2017

Second Printing 2022
ISBN: 978-1-7322673-6-7
Published by Tina Erwin

DISCLAIMER: The contents of this publication are intended for educational and informative use only. They are not to be considered directive nor as a guide to self-diagnosis or self-treatment. Before embarking on any therapeutic regimen, it is absolutely essential that you consult with and obtain the approval of your personal physician or health care provider.

Cover Design by Tina Erwin

Other Works by Tina Erwin

The Lightworker's Guide to Healing Grief
The Lightworker's Guide to Everyday Karma
Ghost Stories from the Ghosts' Point of View Vol. 1
Ghost Stories from the Ghosts' Point of View Vol. 2
Ghost Stories from the Ghosts' Point of View Vol. 3
Soul Evolution: Past Lives and Karmic Ties
The Crossing Over Prayer Book

The GhostHelper App

IV

TABLE OF CONTENTS

VIII

ACKNOWLEDGEMENTS

I was once told that I 'collect' people, that I find so many people so interesting that they become part of my life because I enjoy each of them so much. I think we all collect people on our karmic path, and some of them can be a tremendous asset to you along the way.

This is especially true for this book. This book enables me to share these ancient concepts with a modern-day perspective to people all over the world. But this information takes coordinated assistance. I am deeply grateful to my sister, Andrea Harris for sharing her experiences in grief and karma, and her editorial work. Thank you also to my niece Marisa Harris for enabling me to be able to upload this book!

My brother Pierre Debs was instrumental in helping to educate me, in the often mysterious, ways of karma. My brother Paul Debs has been a loyal supporter, challenging me with probing questions and poignant examples of karma in action.

I am also very grateful to my family, especially my very patient husband, who has been supportive of this hard work in creating the radio show, podcasts, and now books.

Tina Erwin

My daughter and daughters-in-law who have helped with editing, and other aspects of getting these books published, Jeanne Marie, Amee, and Monica.

I am grateful to all my friends who have attended the many evenings I have offered to discuss the nuances of metaphysics. I called the group Light Times because I wanted to keep the energy fun, filled with enlightenment and insight. My heart-filled thanks go out to all of these lovely people who came to share my path.

And thank you to all who read these books and who may begin to look at the world in a different way. May you walk with the angels along your karmic path.

INTRODUCTION

This book is designed to be a supplement to my previous GhostHelper radio shows and podcasts. The concept of karma is not new. It is as old as the universe. My goal with this book, is to open people to new perspectives and ideas. It is my intention to help people understand and recognize that every behavior, action, or reaction affects many things and people around us. The love, compassion, and caring we send to others echoes out, and so does hate, intolerance, anger, and fear. These energies, or frequencies, bombard us all day long. No one escapes it. If we can take a moment to be mindful before we act or react to a situation, we can begin to change our karmic paths for the better. We can even capitalize on the ripple effect that we send out.

This book discusses karma in depth and how the concept of frequency, energy, or chi applies to karma.

As we consciously embark on our karmic or spiritual path, we will gain new insights and knowledge that will help us on our journeys.

The power of intention is one of the key factors on this journey. Someone cuts us off when we are driving. We have a choice: we can become angry and send out anger, or we can do something worse. Or maybe we pause, and take a moment, and send love to that driver. Maybe that driver is having a really bad day. Another example of the power of intention is when we perform those often, mundane tasks, like cooking. When a meal is prepared with love, it simply tastes better. The vibration or energy around the meal table echoes out, nourishing on many levels. Because everything has a vibration or energetic frequency, we need to trust our instincts, intuition, or gut feelings. Have you ever been around a certain person and found that you felt absolutely drained when you left? The opposite can also be true. You come across an old friend, reconnect, and feel super energized. How does that happen? And it is not just people that carry this energetic vibration. Locations can also leave us feeling great or not so great.

This book is an in-depth explanation of these concepts: the cause and effect of the ripples we are making all around us and impacting each other, for better or worse.

THE KARMIC PATH CONCEPT

Drop a pebble in still waters. Watch the corresponding ripple effect that glides out in 360° of energetic reaction to the introduction of that one single pebble.

The 'dropping' of that pebble is the *action*.

The 'ripple' effect of that pebble is the *reaction*.

This is karma.

We are all dropping pebbles in the karmic pool that defines the lives we are living, whether we are conscious of it or not. All our actions are creating an energetic ripple effect throughout time and space every moment we live, and all of those ripples are colliding with the ripples from other dropped pebbles.

This is why karma is complicated, because we are constantly impacting other people whom we do not know.

Sometimes we drop a pebble in the pool and sometimes

we toss a boulder in that pool. The size and degree of action and reaction inevitably determine our moment-by-moment karmic path through this and future lives.

Karma, the Sanskrit term, is also a basic law of physics that notes that for every action, there is an equal and opposite result. Whatever we do, whatever actions we take will have some type of corresponding and fated effect. The original purpose of the Ghosthelpers podcast series, is to provide the tools and the insight to enable all of us to be more mindful of every single pebble or boulder we are dropping into that energetic pool of life. Our actions affect all of those around us in either a neutral, beneficial, or detrimental manner. Many times, we may not know the effect our actions will have on others. However, there are those instances when we do know without a shred of doubt, that the very next action we take will have a huge impact on another person and that impact will inevitably ripple, ricochet or echo back to us.

As you read this book and/or are listening to a podcast, hopefully, you will awaken to an entirely new world of understanding and empowerment to enable you to grow emotionally and spiritually.

May we all be ever mindful of our words and actions as we each walk our own personal karmic paths.

PART I
WHAT IS KARMA?

We have all heard the word karma and the phrases that accompany any description of karma, such as:

"*What goes around comes around.*"

"Justice will be served eventually even though that bad guy didn't get convicted. I have to believe that."

"He'll get what's coming to him."

"No good deed goes unrewarded."

"You reap what you sow."

"Wish I could be there when he meets his maker."

"Another sleazy politician got caught – finally."

You can look at your actions like a karmic savings and loan: you bank good karma, and you borrow against that karma when you do detrimental things.

Are these phrases describing karma? What do they really mean? And where did they come from? Almost everyone has a story where they witnessed 'instant karma'. You are on the freeway and an aggressive driver cuts you off and you witness him cutting off others and speeding down the freeway as if he owns it and is the only person on the road. You become fearful for your safety and the safety of those around you. Then about a mile or two later, you see his car off the road. He did not navigate the turn, or his tire blew out. Something happened and you may never know what that was, but you know that he is now experiencing a dose of instant karma: his car is mangled. The police will probably cite him for reckless diving. Those around him are fortunate to not have been in an accident that he caused. At times, karma is not so instant but as it plays out, you may witness someone around you who experiences a huge 'karmic payout'. It could be that friendly neighbor who is always helpful, spending his time in the garage tinkering around with something. Yet, when your child's tire became flat, he stopped what he was doing to help him. Perhaps he constantly checks in on an elderly neighbor, making minor house repairs for someone who no longer can. Then one day, you hear that the project he has worked on for years in his garage was patented and he just sold it for a million dollars. You think to yourself, "Finally, one of the good guys has won!" And you are happy for him.

Karma is a Sanskrit term for action, reaction, work, or

deed. Karma defines the spiritual law of physics that states categorically that for every action there is an equal and opposite reaction.

Understanding karma means that we begin at the beginning: at the universe level, the macrocosm. But what is the beginning of the universe? The laws of karma govern the entire universe. Karma applies to all stars, black holes, planets, and heavenly bodies in the vast expanse that defines the Universe. It applies to all levels of human consciousness and all types of development on all worlds. It governs The One, The Whole. It governs All That Is. This is the **macrocosm** of karma.

The **microcosm** is how karma applies to each of us every day. Karma in one word represents the Law of Consequences. This is the law that reminds us that there is a consequence to every decision we make, or every action that we take, or do not take, neglect, ignore or hope will go away. Whatever we do – or don't do – has a consequence, either sooner, or later. Hence, all energy is the same – how it is used is the determining factor in all actions, thoughts, and deeds and ultimately - consequence.

A ready example would be the use of fire.

Strike a match.

That one little match can light a fireplace that warms your home, or it can be used to burn down your house. The energy of fire has not changed: the use of fire is all that changes and as you can readily see, each action with that match carries a completely different karmic reaction.

The word karma literally means 'action,' and karma is both the power latent with actions and the 'reaction,' or results our actions bring.

We rely on karma for the fabric of everyday living. Day unceasingly folds into night just as surely as birth and death trade places in our lives and the lives of those around us. We seek the security of law and order, of that indefinable sense of justice that we *must*
trust with all our hearts when all too often injustice seems to rule the short-term view of our moments.

THE LAW OF KARMA

What does karma mean? It means that whatever we do, with our body, speech, or mind, creates a corresponding result. All cultures have an understanding of the Law of Karma, and to help us make sense of this concept we commonly hear phrases like the ones below:

"Do unto others as you would have them do unto you."
"Whatever you do, comes back to you."
"What goes around comes around."
*"As you sow, so **shall** you reap."*
"An eye for an eye."

Karma is God. God, the bringer of justice and of balance is the ultimate aspect of this great law. There are two aspects of God's karmic Law of Consequence. The elegant logic that is God, offers a variety of experiences for each soul as the individual walks his or her karmic path.

When a soul disregards the basic laws of humanity, of moral law that has unfailingly been laid out for all of us, then this person will encounter a most difficult karmic pattern. That challenging karmic path is the direct result of arrogantly ignoring the life laws that have unfailingly been laid out for all of us, to follow.

If a drug user kills a child in the commission of a robbery trying to gain money for his drug habit, what is his karma? Should the drug dealer be executed or face life in prison because murder was committed in the robbery? Will life in prison or execution clear the karma of this action? What is the karma of the child to be killed in this way? What if the drug dealer who committed the murder is never caught? How is justice served? Justice is served in ways we will never know, may never see and may not be able to understand.

Now consider that a baby could be born drug addicted. The possibility exists that the child could have been a drug user or dealer in a previous life and now experiences the return of his or her actions, and while this is a hard concept to embrace, karma can be returned this way. This is why we may never know how it all comes back to us or anyone else.

Then there are 'factors in mitigation' despite our believing that mortal justice is a classic example of how karma is supposed to work. We often believe this justice is black and white. Someone steals something. The thief is caught with the stolen goods and the thief is then sent to prison. But what if the thief is a child, stealing food to survive? Should a ten-year old go to prison for stealing bread? What if a teenager is stealing money to help his or her family to survive? How does karma look at this? Should this person go to prison or are there factors in mitigation, meaning, is there more to the story that will affect the application of karmic and moral justice?

The positive karmic path is the result of following the moral, ethical, and natural laws of the universe, of nature and of basic human decency. When a soul demonstrates courage, bravery, sacrifice, tremendous service, hope and deep and profound love for his or her fellow human beings, then this person has laid out a most positive karmic experience. Some souls return to perform ever-greater levels of service in life after life. Mother Theresa may have been one such soul. Her dedication to service provided a global example of the good that can be done for humanity. Her next life will offer even greater opportunities to help mankind since this would seem to be her soul path: helping the world learn the day-to-day meaning of compassion and kindness.

Even if a soul encountered difficulty while adhering to

this path in one life, that soul will be rewarded in the next life. The soul could also find that adherence to the path of a positive life could also afford him or her beneficial things in the current life. It is difficult to know how and when karma can or will be balanced. The karmic wheel, of course is never bound by merely one life. **Each karmically positive life takes that soul closer to stepping beyond the reincarnation cycle of life/death and moving more permanently into life in the Heaven World.**

GOD IS NOT PUNISHING US

Why is it then, with such a purely simple law, that people still think that when bad things happen to them that it is 'God's retribution?' Or when they win the lottery, that it is luck, or God smiling upon them? Perhaps the answer lies in our, often human, reluctance to accept responsibility for our actions, thoughts, ideas, and creations. Once this concept is taken to heart, then we are now responsible. We cannot go back and claim ignorance that we did not know or understand and say that it is God's fault. We understand that we are responsible for our actions. Perhaps actions can be understood, but what about words, ideas, or thoughts? How do these come back to us?

Can't we have even private moments where we are

angry? Yes, of course, but the fundamental element of karma is how we choose to act or not to act on those thoughts.

We may not always feel that the laws of man, or day-to-day life are just, but the law of karma is always just, and always balanced. Even though a person may be seeking that negative power experience for the sheer aspect of the dominance over others that comes from it, ultimately if the soul learns from that dark moment and changes his or her life in a positive way, then karma can be changed in the future. That would be an element of a desire for atonement, which again changes that individual's karmic future.

Consider the schoolyard bully. If he or she is able to recognize their behavior and its consequences later in life and then seek to atone for these actions, karma can move in the direction of balance.

WHAT ARE EQUAL REACTIONS?

When you show kindness to someone, kindness will be shown to you.

When you show someone your anger, cruelty or lack of ethics, those same aspects will be shown to you. Someone may then cheat you, may be angry or cruel toward you.

If everywhere you go you meet the nicest people, then

it will be a result of how well you are treating others.

If the world 'sucks' for you, are you making the world 'suck' for those around you: are they simply responding to you?

If you chose to examine your actions in any particular life, if that level of precious insight were to awaken in you and you chose to do some modest level of service in one life, then the next life will offer even greater opportunities to use newly acquired skills and abilities. So literally, the better student you are of karma in one life, the more you will come to understand it, embrace it, and share it in the next life when you reincarnate.

Reincarnation is a process of learning to evolve into a spiritual being by living life after mortal life in learning the lessons of experience. That process can take many thousands of lives to realization.

You will be afforded greater and greater opportunities life after life until eventually, you no longer have any need to reincarnate: your mortal lessons will have all been learned. Then, you will be offered new paths to higher levels of evolution on the spiritual realm.

Who controls your karmic actions? You control your own karma – you are the master of your own fate, the captain of your own ship. Karma is not predetermined. Every single day you live you have free will in how you will react with every encounter you have with the people in your life, with nature and with your sense of ethics, and how you treat your body. You will never which lifetime will be your last one.

You own your future. **You create your future, minute-by-minute, day-by-day, century-by-century and lifetime after lifetime.** And in every moment, you are influencing those around you with every single decision you make, just as they are influencing **you** by every single decision **they** make.

Beginning now, in this moment, you can change your own future by agreeing, and deciding to make positive changes. Even seemingly negative situations, events that break your heart are still filled with opportunities to learn, to change, and to grow. Dark situations can make you become dark if *you allow it to become so*. You can also make a different choice: learning from the situation, deciding to change your own personal outcome. You may not ever be able to change what happened, but you can surely change how you will face the world for the rest of your life. You can choose to be bitter and angry or decide to offer the world the best of yourself and show hope, fortitude, and courage as you face the days ahead.

THE TRUE POWER OF WORDS AND THOUGHTS

Thoughts are forms of energy. Every great structure or event or invention began as a *thought*. Therefore, thoughts are energy and this 'thought form' energy has tremendous power. Hence, if you think something truly bad about another person, that thought is negative power sent to that person. The power of thought creates action, feelings or deeds, and this power creates karma.

"Sticks and stones can break my bones, but words can never hurt me." How tragically wrong this statement is. Words are deadlier than any spear, bullet, poison, or knife. Words are insidious in their destructive ability, because when anyone says something about another, they send the power/energy of those words to that person. The person hears those words on many levels: consciously and subconsciously. The violence of negative words can destroy a person. The power of positive words can carry a person to the greatest heights.

This point is critical. Negative words become a form of violence directed toward a person and this violence results in the weight of negative karma. Conversely, positive words, meaningfully and honestly said carry the weight of positive karma.

A case in point involves anorexia. Perhaps some of you remember the tragic case of the singer, Karen Carpenter. Early in the career of the singing group 'The Carpenters,' it was believed that a newspaper reporter made a written comment about "Richard's chubby little sister, Karen. . ." From that point on, Karen went on a crusade to be thin and eventually starved herself to death. Did the reporter put a gun to her head? Did he refuse her food? Did he *intend* to harm her? The answer to those questions is no. Does he bear some responsibility for her death? There would appear to be a possible connection. We are not here to judge the reporter, only to illustrate the effect of words. There may also have been other emotional issues that were simply exacerbated by the reporter's comment. We will never know for sure. Karen also had a choice: she could have chosen to reject those words and break free of any labels.

Parenting is a tremendous responsibility. Parents unwittingly commit verbal and thought violence against their children. This is particularly insidious because the subconscious of a child *absolutely believes* the words of a parent - the parent is 'like a god' to a child. When a parent tells a child that he or she is fat, dumb, ugly, and good for nothing, the parent is always surprised when the child grows up to be just that. These same parents look with envy at the children of other parents who tell their children *daily, in an appropriate context that they are* intelligent, gentle, kind, beautiful, and worthwhile people. These parents are not at all surprised when their children grow up to be great people. You reap what you sow, especially with children. You get out of children that which you put into them: garbage in, garbage out: goodness in, goodness out. The positive karma created by telling/teaching a child how to be a positive person is returned to the parent in a form of richness of happiness beyond calculation.

When your words or deeds seek power over another person because of your own insecurity, you are still perpetrating violence against that person. This is illustrated in various personality types:

Passive Aggressive - The 'passive aggressive' person is usually indirectly aggressive by being stubborn or procrastinating. This chronic behavior creates frustration and anger in others. The passive aggressive person knows that their behavior is a tool to manipulate people. On some level, the person is aware of it, yet continues to practice those behaviors. This can be changed with intent.

Interrogator - We have all met the 'Interrogator' personality. This teacher, parent, boss, sibling, or friend endlessly points out another person's failings. With an interrogator personality, you will never get it right, and will never be good enough. The military has a name for it: faint praise - "you would have gotten it perfect except. . ." "If only you had. . ." "Well, I would have. . ." Ask yourself if you say these things to people.

Intimidator - The "Intimidator" personality perpetrates violence by creating fear in those around them with their unending threats and criticism. You often see this in a mother who never disciplines her children. Instead, she threatens her children with "Wait 'til your father gets home, and he'll really punish you." The father then believes the mother and blindly punishes the children. The children wait in terror all day long. The meek, spineless mother becomes a terrible bully to her children. Another example is the boss who threatens employees with doing the same task over and over, for the sheer power of micromanaging those around them. This boss creates unending fear and stress in his or her staff. Parents, friends, and managers who criticize constantly also create an environment of failure. Ask yourself if you say or do these things to your family or employees.

No one likes the above feelings. Doing these things to others is a power and control drama that can create negative karma. Constructive observation focuses on building not on destroying another person.

DOES KARMA APPLY TO THE PHYSICAL BODY?

Yes. You often hear of children being born with terrible diseases such as cancer, deformities, or mental challenges. These situations are often the unfortunate result or expression of past karma. The more diligently the child and family work to help that person heal emotionally and physically, the more that past karma can be readily overcome.

Each of us has a unique responsibility to take care of our physical body in a loving and gentle way. Our self-image is critical to the care of the body.

If we work to create a positive self-image through proper diet, exercise, a clean and healthy environment, and positive surroundings and manageable stress, then we create varying degrees of beneficial karma.

Perhaps the best example is an individual's health in

old age. The actions of youth are always visited upon our older bodies. The person who, at an early age started taking health supplements, exercising, and caring for the body reaps the positive karma of advanced years free from debilitating illnesses and injuries. If at any time, you choose to change your health karma, then you begin to reverse the negative karma by the degree of change you activate.

Karma also applies to the many lifetimes of the physical body. The more you can clean up or perfect your current DNA, the better, stronger, happier body/DNA you will have in future lives.

IS THE KARMA YOU CREATE IN THIS LIFETIME ALWAYS *SPENT* IN THIS LIFETIME?

Yes and no. The karma you create in this lifetime can readily be returned to you in this lifetime depending on the degree and circumstances of the karma. You don't really know if some small bit of karma will come back to you immediately, which is sometimes called 'instant karma,' or if it will take years or even lifetimes. There are so many factors which play into each situation that it is almost beyond our ability to fathom how this is all calculated, but calculated, managed, and balanced it is.

Many times, the karma you have created over many lifetimes is of such intensity, good or bad, that it can come back to you over many centuries. It is very hard to know what you set in motion by previous deeds. If you are in a position that affects many millions, thousands, hundreds or dozens of people and your actions assist those people, then it may take many lifetimes for that goodness to be returned to you. Examples: Mother Theresa, Mahatma Gandhi, the creators of the United States Constitution, including George Washington, Thomas Jefferson, John Adams, and the other signers, in addition to other wonderful people. It is important to understand that each of these 'wonderful' people may have also had personal flaws or done things in their lifetimes that were not perfect. The overarching element is the sum-total of a person's karma. Unfortunately, the reverse is also true.

It is not normally possible to *know* what you did in previous lives and frankly, not necessary. Each life is a new beginning to mitigate, change or enhance, the karma previously created.

However, if what you did negatively affected the lives of millions, caused suffering to human beings, animals, and nature itself, then this karma must be returned to you as well. It is the law. Those involved with the destruction of nature, which directly affects all people on the planet, can definitely expect this karma to come back to them in this life and for lifetimes to come.

Consider drug dealers who have destroyed the lives of

millions of families in seemingly unimaginable ways or even drug manufacturers who knowingly harm people in a blind effort to make money be it through toxic injectable serums or harmful drugs. The karma of the *conscious decisions made* must be returned to each soul in some balancing way.

WHAT IF YOU INADVERTENTLY CAUSED HARM?

The original inventors of x-rays had no idea that their new device could be harmful. The elements of radiation were unknown. It took time to understand the ramifications of what they created. Once learned, then proper precautions were taken to safeguard people. The greater good offered using x-rays to help the medical establishment heal the body would be offset by the original ignorance and harm of the first x-ray machines used. The karma here is a factor in mitigation.

But what of automobile manufacturers who are repeatedly told that a certain part in their car will cause the vehicle to malfunction and possibly crash? Here is a conscious, karmic crossroads to either: immediately inform their customers and eat the cost or to 'hope the problem will go away.' Yes, some manufacturers ignore it until enough deaths trigger a class-action lawsuit and then government intervention to fix the problem is required. Karma will have to balance the effects of those decisions by those specific individuals. *People make decisions, not corporations. Individuals are always karmically responsible for their actions on every level.* Whistleblowers may feel that their efforts to protect the public are punished, but karma knows the effort it takes to risk everything for the greater good.

Tina Erwin

HOW KARMA AFFECTS YOUR FAMILY NOW AND, IN THE FUTURE

Ever wonder why some families seem to have a history of tragedy and some families have hard and good times, but no intense tragedies? This relates to karma. In many situations, the sins of the ancestors are definitely visited upon future generations. Keep in mind that karma can be changed or mitigated by a change in behavior or good deeds by individual family members. An interesting example has its beginning in the Second World War.

THE KENNEDY LEGACY

William Stevenson wrote a fascinating book titled *A Man Called Intrepid*. It detailed many of the behind-the-scenes actions at the highest levels of the British Government during World War II. One of the most chilling stories he relates describes the actions of the United States Ambassador to Great Britain, Joseph P. Kennedy. Mr. Kennedy turned a curiously blind eye to the relentless, bloody conquest of Europe by Nazi Germany and constantly advised King George VI not to enter the war, to ignore the ruthless carving up of Europe by Hitler and the Nazis. In fact, Kennedy was feeding intelligence information to the Nazis in return for concessions to the rights to British gin and whiskey factories. Mr. Kennedy wanted German assurances that British ships filled with these goods would receive safe passage to the United States. To the absolute horror of then President Roosevelt in 1939, when the British declared war on Germany, Joseph Kennedy actually toasted the Germans whom he unabashedly believed would badly destroy the English. Not long after Mr. Kennedy made his Nazi sympathizer views known, he was recalled as US Ambassador to Great Britain.

The British always felt that Joe Kennedy aided and abetted the Germans in the extermination of the Jews and the carving up of Europe. His Catholic faith seemed to leave him strangely lacking in moral values regarding human life. He did not feel that the laws of humanity applied to him specifically and that, when necessary, he could create his own rules. What karma did he create? Although we are not in a position to know for sure, the tragedies that befell his family including the immediate loss of his oldest son in World War II, and then later, two other sons by way of assassinations, plus the sicknesses, deaths, divorces, and accidents may hopefully stop as future generations continue to do positive things.

Can any family change their pattern? Can they change or mitigate their family karma? All people are capable of changing their karma by good deeds, by changing negative patterns. All that is required is positive action, intent, insight, and remorse for that which has gone before. Perhaps the actions of future generations of Kennedy children will change the family karma. We are affected by the actions of our forefathers, whether we want to believe this or not and yet we have the power to positively change that karma for future generations. Whether you think your family karma is good or bad, all that matters is that your focus is on doing good deeds for yourself and others.

THE DEATH OF BABIES AND SMALL CHILDREN: WHAT WAS THEIR KARMA?

We cannot know their karma. This brings up the point

that it is extremely important not to judge situations that we may observe, especially as they involve children. When a baby dies soon after birth, there are many facets including the aspect that this baby may have only needed a few very short experiences in a particular life. Once these were accomplished, that child left. Was this karma?

Consider that souls live forever. A soul enters a mortal body and leaves a mortal body. The age of that mortal body is incidental and sometimes irrelevant to the growth of a soul. What this means is that when we think of a baby, we think of a new soul, but that soul could be thousands of years old and in this one incarnation this *soul only needed a few short experiences, and then the soul left that baby's body.*

Souls incur karma, whether they are children, adults, or babies. Souls do this, so that when a baby or child dies, we do not know what the karma of that soul was, only that something occurred that had to be balanced in some other way. Also, the death of a child is a karmic manipulation because so many people are affected. This is why understanding karma becomes complicated - we are not allowed to see the 3rd, 4th, or 5th dimensional aspects of the karma of this soul.

Another element may be the karma of the parents in the loss of their child. It may be that the parents were required to show intense love for their child and that this love was critical for that tiny soul. Once the soul received that love, then something was completed, and the soul could leave. Karmic timing determines this, not individuals. Maybe this soul had never fully known unconditional love. When the soul completes what it came here to experience, technically he or she can leave. This can happen at any point in the life of a soul/mortal person. The parents incur karma in how they handle the death of their child both within themselves and between them as a couple. How do they help friends and family members cope with this loss? Every karmic situation offers all parties an opportunity to rise to their highest level of goodness and healing.

There may be those times when the death of a family member provides others in the family the experience of knowing grief, of needing to value human life and each other more each day. Every single death has a purpose, even when any rational explanation seems to elude us.

WHAT ABOUT SUICIDE?

Some people believe that suicide is a terrible sin; some believe it is a sin against God. What if suicide is not a sin? What if suicide is a situation of staggering conflict within a soul, which the soul believes cannot be handled in any other way than by leaving the mortal body? Unless any of us have felt the profound darkness and depression of someone in this situation, none of us are in any position to judge that individual's actions.

Understanding the karma here is complicated. Once the soul has died, he or she is almost always remorseful for the emotional pain and sorrow they have unintentionally inflicted on their friends and families. However, it is important to understand that *they felt they had no other option.*

The truth is, this trapped feeling drove them over the edge of rational thought. Their depression and aloneness could have been something they felt no one else on earth would ever understand. These souls never intended to hurt their families. The sad irony is that now their family members instantly rush to the closet and put on a cloak of guilt that they never take off for the rest of their lives. This is unnecessary, and only increases the pain of the soul who took his or her life.

The more slowly a person poisons their body the less it is considered deliberate and the more accepted their death becomes. Sudden suicide is rejected as a terrible act, but slow suicide through alcohol or drug addiction is less obvious. Perhaps we should all shift our perspective.

The follow-on issue is how each living family member handles the aftermath of a suicide experience. Guilt is a powerful factor, a cruel emotion that can color all the rest of a person's days. One woman, whose sister committed suicide felt that she could never forgive herself for her sister's death. She had convinced herself that despite years of efforts to assist her severely drug-addicted sister, she could have done more to prevent her suicide. The truth is, that if a person looks at an emotionally charged situation with even a slight level of detachment, they will come to realize that sometimes, the soul *will never allow you to help them preclude suicide*. Guilt seeks punishment and many a life-threatening illness has taken its toll on a guilty family member *("I should have done something to prevent that suicide")* even if this sentiment was never true. Most of the time, there is very little that any family member can do to stop a person from ending his or her own life.

The karma of ending one's life is never black and white. Sudden death in this manner does create karma but then all deaths by any means create karma. If a soul felt so tortured that suicide was the only option, who are we to judge the desperate release that person sought from that pain? They honestly believed that death would free them from their emotional prison. As we release judgment of their action, we can allow ourselves to remember that there is no 'sin' here only the experience of leaving early. Karma will handle this soul and what will come next for them. It is not ours to judge.

The soul had a profound experience. If the soul is assisted in crossing into the Heaven World, (by using the prayers at the end of this book and in ***The Crossing Over Prayer Book***©) then he or she will receive healing for the life just lived, and guidance for future lives. If the soul does not cross over, then when the soul reincarnates then he or she may commit suicide life after life, as the following example illustrates.

There is the interesting story of a beautiful, dark haired, young woman named Callie, who was in the process of divorcing her current husband and sought spiritual counseling to help her deal with her divorce. In the course of time, this young woman had several past life regressions. In every single life, an event happened where a particular person died. In one life it was her father, in another, her son and in a third life, it was her husband in this life. She felt chilled to learn, that the person who died each time, *was the same soul* (meaning that the same soul, the same person returned life after life to offer her the experience of his death). In each life, she killed herself soon after this person died. In fact, in the last life, she committed suicide within hours of his death.

She wondered what she should learn from these regressions. Her counselor advised her that she kept having the same experience over and over, life after life because karma could see that she was not learning the lesson of accepting the death of this particular soul. They worked through her trauma in each of those lives, helping her to understand the concepts of attachment and the need to release the soul who died.

After some months, their sessions ceased. Within months of these sessions ending, Callie met a handsome Marine pilot while traveling on an airplane. It was love at first sight, (probably because he was the soul who kept dying in those previous lives). Their engagement and wedding were in the final planning stages when the love of her life died in a plane crash. Her grief and despair were so tremendous that she immediately contemplated suicide. But she knew that she had to stop repeating this action, so she called her adviser and began the critical process of working through her grief.

It took months of spiritual work, even beyond grief work. Consequently, Callie did not take her life this time. She stopped her sessions and began to successfully move on with her life.

One day, roughly a year later, her counselor received a beautiful wedding invitation in the mail announcing the marriage of Callie and another handsome Marine pilot. Her counselor called her and asked her how she was doing. She said she was doing extremely well and told her counselor how important her presence would be at this wedding.

"You are the only person in the world who will know, that as I walk down that aisle, I am changing centuries of self-destructive patterns. I need you to be there, to silently celebrate with me my progress in soul evolution."

Her wedding was lovely, and she married a wonderful

man and as the years went by, they developed a great relationship. However, her longing for the love of her life never left her although she was able to control her desire to leave. Souls who seek to evolve show great courage, sometimes in simply living every day.

It is critical to note in the example above that Callie was "not punished by God." Karma can be extremely compassionate. What she was repeatedly given was the opportunity to change her spiritual and karmic path. When she was finally ready to make that critical change, a teacher was placed in front of her. When a student is ready a teacher will be there. Once she learns this critical life lesson, then this type of experience may not ever have to be repeated. My sincerest hope is that in a future life, she and this wonderful man will be able to have an entire lifetime of happiness together.

WHAT ABOUT MURDER?

If a person commits murder - does that mean that they will be murdered in another life? Perhaps, but karma is never that simple. 'An eye for an eye' is never that blatant.

The results of karmic actions in one lifetime are often delayed for future lifetimes and then the murderer may not necessarily be murdered but may experience another challenging situation that may or may not cause death. If the person returned in a future lifetime, and cleaned up their act, devoted himself or herself to a life of service, then they begin to mitigate the karma that was created by the murder that they committed in a previous life. Karma can offer such blessings and opportunities. There is no good luck or bad fortune: there is only karma and how it is returned to each of us.

If someone murdered you in a previous lifetime and you meet them in this lifetime, there is a high probability that the souls may have a 'knowing' of each other. They will not necessarily know that this event occurred but will have an uneasy *feeling* about each other. What is happening is that their subconscious selves recognize each other and remember the feeling of the murderous act from that past life experience. This is why some people just hate each other at first sight, despite having no specific prior personal history in this lifetime to generate such an intense emotion. You are put together again because you did not quite get it right in the last life. How extraordinary that we get another chance. You have a choice to try to work things out with this person, forgive yourself and that other person and feel peace among you. This can happen, it does happen, and it is in these wonderful instances that spiritual progress is made. It means that you are finally evolving. Unfortunately, the reverse is also true - people just keep killing each other life after life, or hating each other, and the old patterns frequently remain unbroken, whether people realize it or not.

Sometimes there is no choice, you just have to accept that *something happened between you, and either avoid that person or try to work through it the best you can.*

I remember hearing a story of a woman name Joan who had a past life regression. She had always had an extreme dislike for her mother-in-law Carol and wanted to understand why. What she clearly saw was that Carol, her mother-in-law in this lifetime, was also her mother-in-law from a previous life in the late 1600s. Carol had caused her daughter-in-law Joan's murder all those centuries ago by declaring that Joan was a witch and Joan was executed for witchcraft. These two women must have had multiple lifetimes of intense difficulty that may have culminated in the murder of the young wife in that lifetime. Joan's husband in the 1600s' (and ironically, her current husband) was powerless to stop his mother from falsely testifying and causing the murder his wife. Fast forward to the 20th century. Karma, being always efficient, places all the same players *together again, sometimes, even in the same roles.* Now what happens when these two women meet each other for the first time? The mother-in-law instantly hates her son's fiancé, and the fiancé throws up at meeting her mother-in-law to be. They so loathe each other that the son does not know what to do. Eventually, after the couple marries, they cut off all contact with this hateful mother-in-law. Years pass. The couple seeks out a spiritual practitioner to help them understand this mother-in-law (who was intractable) and to help them to find spiritual balance with her.

However, because the couple's intention is to try to heal this relationship in this lifetime, miraculous things begin to happen. After roughly fourteen years of no contact, all the parties are able to manage an accommodation with established ground rules that enable them to have some sort of limited relationship with this mother-in-law. The mother-in-law softens. The daughter-in-law softens. No one dies violently in this lifetime. There is peace among them all. Karma will definitely smile on this situation. However, this was not an easy challenge for the couple to resolve, but they stuck with it and all parties have earned karmic brownie points for their karmic bank account, in the process.

HOLOCAUSTS AND GROUP KARMA

Most of us find it hard to understand the karmic actions that took place during the Holocaust in Germany in World War II. This was surely group karma, but why? Before seeking to answer this truly difficult question, consider all the other 'Holocausts' that have taken place:

•Pol Pot's massacre of almost the entire country of Laos.

•The Chinese Communist repression after World War

II where up to 15 million people were killed.

•Stalin's pogroms and murders, where many more millions were also murdered.

•The slaughter of the American Indians by disease and violence when the white man arrived in North America.

•The horror of the Africans at the hands of black slave traders where the weak were slaughtered and many thousands more were enslaved by whites.

•The destruction of Tibet by Chinese Communists in more modern times.

No culture, country, sect, religion, people, or group of people has a monopoly on suffering. The higher the number, the more difficult it is to fathom. Why vast numbers of people die at once is not fully understood, but in some way, their deaths were a type of mass group karma, not currently fully understood, but in some way, their deaths were part of karma.

When we are face to face with staggering evil, the energy of defeating this evil is not wasted and earns karma. People who suffer, people who fight to free those suffering and those who do not fight, but who remain behind and pray, earn karma. These are tremendous factors that bring balance and hope to any situation. Remembering the aftermath of evil is also a karmic responsibility.

We are reminded that God does not harm us. We harm ourselves and sow the seeds of future happiness or tragedy. Karma is never unfair - it is always balanced. We create the horrors, and we also have freedom of choice to prevent future horrors.

Group karma was also created after WWII when the allies *did not perpetuate the same mistake that was made after WWI: punishing the German people.* This time, they helped to rebuild both Germany and Japan so that these countries could become allies and never make war with the rest of the world again. This level of insight created tremendous positive karma possibly helping to mitigate the potential for a third world war.

REINCARNATION, HEREDITY AND GROUP KARMA

There can be no discussion of karma without a very specific discussion of reincarnation. We live life after life after life after life for the experiences and the opportunities to burn off past negative karmic reactions and/or to create new positive karmic reactions and actions. Karma cannot exist for mortal souls without reincarnation: reincarnation *is karma.*

Group karma can be many things. A family is group karma: you choose to be together to gain experiences, to work things out, for souls to understand one another better, to gain and give forgiveness. A family that dies together in an auto or plane accident is also an example of group karma.

Tina Erwin

When we are born, we join a specific family because we have very specific energetic and karmic ties to that family created from various past lives and past karma. Karma is hope made manifest. If your beloved child, parent, spouse, or friend died in this lifetime, karma and reincarnation offer you the hope, the surety that you will see this soul again and perhaps in a future life, have a longer experience with that person.

But the reverse is also true. If someone was abused or was the abuser in a past lifetime, then both abuser and the abused will return again to have the opportunity to work out what was not resolved in that past life. Sadly, most people never take this step, but the opportunity is always present.

This is why we have very powerful feelings about some people. Perhaps love at first sight is merely instant soul recognition, rejoicing at meeting an adored person again and having a new opportunity with that person. Karma, being ever efficient, also shows us that we have instant fear and trepidation about some people upon first meeting him or her. We do not trust that person because of something terrible that this person did to us in a past life. It is not necessary to remember what it was; we only have to acknowledge that feeling.

Being with someone who was negative in a past life (whether you are aware of that previous life or not,) offers all the parties the opportunity to work off past

42

negative karma and at the same time create truly wonderful karma in this life, paving the way for different and perhaps more sophisticated karmic experiences in future lives.

Families are inherently group karma in action, and the dramas that exist in families if positively worked out, can be tremendously beneficial. Sometimes the lesson is for one family member to separate themselves from family members who are not making any efforts toward resolving their chronic negative karmic patterns. In these cases, the person must leave the family to have any chance at building positive karma. The toxic energies of a family can cause a soul to continue down a dark path. Separating, *learning the lesson from the family* by *leaving* that family can mean that you have broken that terrible karmic pattern. Some stubborn souls never learn. That does not have to be your path, but it takes profound courage to strike out on that new path. Ironically, as lonely as it may at first appear, people will come along to help you.

What about natural disasters, such as tornadoes, hurricanes, train, or plane crashes where everyone dies but one person or a few people? What is that karma? Karmically it was not his or her time to die. The soul had the karma to be there but not necessarily to die there. This is also true in wartime situations where veterans have survivor guilt. "Why did I live, and everyone else die?" The answer is purely karma: it was not your karma to die, and it was not their karma to live. Sounds harsh, but karma is neither harsh nor sweet. Karma is fair, balanced and just. Perhaps certain people survived while trying to help others, ignoring their own potential peril. Courage is karmically rewarded even if the soul dies, the energy of the courage that soul displayed will be returned at a future time.

NO ENERGY IS EVER WASTED OR THE LAW OF KARMA

Perhaps you have heard this statement before. But what does it mean? Since energy is neither created nor destroyed, then when you spend energy in a positive way, it **has** to come back to you in a positive way and if you spend energy in a negative way, it **has** to come back to you in a negative way. This is also the Law of Karma.

Every single little thing that any of us does will come back to us. No action is too small to go unnoticed by the Law of Karma. The actions that create karma, once set in motion, do not ever stop, like the ringing of a bell, the echo will move through time and space for eternity.

Consider that one tiny spark can destroy an entire building and the seemingly inconsequential dripping of water can eventually create massive damage. Conversely, those tiny drops of water can fill a lake, or a dam and that spark of fire can warm a home.

Karma is not dependent on time, space, or dimension (which will be explained later in this section.) Karma does not dissipate or decay. The strength of each action remains as strong as the moment it was initiated. Neither will time forget it, fire destroy it, or water erode it. Karma is immune to destruction.

While karma cannot be destroyed, it can be balanced, mitigated, and brought to fruition when the right moment presents itself. This means that if you have been given a karmic opportunity to resolve something in the past and you ignored it, you will be given multiple opportunities until you do face it and resolve it. **The challenge here is that each new opportunity may become more challenging than the last, more difficult.**

Be aware that every thought is pregnant with consequence. If you send out angry thoughts - angry thoughts go to the person: you have incurred negative karma. If you send prayers to benefit someone, positive thoughts go to that person, as long as you have not prayed that this person changes to be the person that you want them to be. The correct karmic action is to send loving thoughts to them without denying that soul's free will. Now you have incurred positive karma.

SERVICE CREATES GOOD KARMA

The more service we do in each lifetime the greater the bountiful karmic opportunity is created for the future. If a person does great service in one lifetime, then this person may be offered an opportunity to perform even greater service in future lifetimes. This can be especially powerful once the soul begins to feel the full measure of the joy of helping others.

Service definitely creates wonderful karma - if it is done in balance. This is often a difficult point to understand. What about monks or nuns, or priests or missionaries? Surely these are the best examples of people creating wonderful karma. Perhaps, but if their life is not balanced, then they did not fully learn the lessons they came here to learn. Being cloistered in a monastery does not offer opportunities to learn to get along with the opposite sex or deal with day-to-day problems - it can appear that the person is in fact running away from their problems - just cannot deal with them and "hides out" in a cloistered environment. This is not necessarily negative karma because while they are there, they have the opportunity to learn lessons, and do good deeds, but they have put off other lessons that could have been learned in this lifetime.

If missionaries, in their zeal to spread their belief system end up destroying another culture or hurting others, this may not be considered good karma because they inherently judged another culture and found it wanting. Who put them in charge? Who told them that they could deny the faith of another?

What of nuns and monks, or priests and ministers who abuse their religious power? Abuse of power is not exclusive to the military, politics, or industry; power dramas are everywhere, especially in the world of religion. I long remember the cruelty of many nuns in the Catholic Church I attended as a child, and one verbally abusive priest. Perhaps those religious people in their power dramas thought they were doing the right thing, but cruelty cannot create positive karma. Children who become terrified of a vengeful God have been robbed of the healing power of faith or the comfort of compassion. **Priests and ministers who sexually abuse children incur horrific karma. This is because, they not only terrify, intimidate and abuse, they also commit the ultimate sin: <u>separating the child from God.</u>** The pure evil of these priests, nuns, and ministers, destroys the faith that children have in people professing to be spiritual authorities. Those religious people in their hideous theft of innocence and faith earn a very unique level of negative karma because *they are in the ultimate position of trust, and they know better.* No matter how many times one priest or nun confesses their sins to another priest, no matter how many "Hail Marys" they say, their karma is not mitigated by these "going through the motions" actions. We will never know when or how their karma will be returned to them, *but it will be returned to them,* because karma has eternal memory of all souls in all lifetimes.

If someone is truly repentant, then their process of atonement for past actions can begin in that lifetime through prayer, and positive powerful actions.

Service that creates martyrs is also not creating necessarily positive karma. Part of the issue here is the initial intention of the problematic service performed. Again, if your service is used to avoid lessons, then karma is not fooled. It is like the physician who devotes himself to his patients but ignores his family, or the scientist who works night and day to develop some new breakthrough, but completely hides from facing the death of a dying family member or a mentally impaired child. If your service puts you out of balance with the other important aspects of your life - and you know it and refuse to face it – then although you are doing service, it is mitigated by the refusal to learn lessons when offered.

What about those in the service fields such as nurses, physicians, police, firemen, social/hospice workers - are they always performing service? Yes, but if they have the opportunity to demonstrate compassion or true help and they do not, then they have not created especially positive karma. Sometimes persons in this field become numb to the plight of those very people they are trying to help. Consider the police officer more interested in bringing in money for his police department and corrupts his position by citing motorists for violations he or she never committed. Or the physician who knows how dangerous a injectable serum or drug is for his patient but administers it anyway, thereby causing deliberate harm. Karma has an extremely long memory in these cases: it never forgets.

Karma is like Santa Claus: it sees you when you're sleeping and knows when you are truly of service or when you are in it for yourself. It knows all your thoughts: the greedy and the altruistic ones.

PSYCHIC ABILITY, FORTUNE TELLING AND THE LAW OF KARMA

The entire the population has psychic ability. However, a few people have worked on developing that ability to increase their own personal power. This energy can then be used for either good or bad purposes. There is far greater karmic responsibility for that psychic spiritual practitioner than for the person who just "gets a feeling" about something. Once that spiritual practitioner, intuitive, or psychic is aware of how spiritual laws work, there is no going back to pretending he or she does not know. Hence their actions take on a far greater karmic burden and have significant ramifications because they know on karmically spiritual levels what they are doing.

This is why 'dabbling' is extremely dangerous. Dabbling in magic means that you are doing the Ouija board at a party or becoming heavily addicted to dark video games. It can also mean that you are seeking out spells to use on other people to influence them to do what you want them to do. Dabbling can also mean making use of fortunetellers and questionable psychics. One of the most dangerous forms of dabbling is 'playing' with Tarot cards. Anytime you use any type of card for divination, you are creating varying levels of negative karma, and this *includes all those supposedly harmless angel cards*.

Any time you arrogantly think that you can use these tools or devices, such as cards, games or spells and not have karma return to nip you in the 'tush,' you are mistaken. You can create terrible situations, hurt others and create horrendous karma by using these devices.

This need to be careful was tragically illustrated by a woman who was deliberately practicing the 'dark arts.' She had many powerful devices hidden away in her home. She took delight in putting 'spells' on people, manipulating them and creating vicious and cruel situations. She presented herself as an ordinary mom, but she had a chillingly evil side. One day her daughter found her mom's stash of black magic devices and cards and began to use them. In a short period of time, her daughter died. The woman was devastated by her daughter's death. Why did her daughter die? Was it to show her mother the power of the dark side by letting her feel that towering grief with the loss of a child? Did karma collapse on this mom for the evil she had perpetrated against so many other people?

What about fortune telling, Tarot Readings and Ouija Boards? There are thousands of people performing psychic readings every day using these tools. How does karmic law affect these psychics? We all have freedom of choice. However, when a person goes to a psychic and asks for a reading, this client is automatically giving up a certain amount of free will. This is because the subconscious of the client believes that the psychic is in a position of authority and therefore has knowledge that is credible. This may or may not be true, but a certain amount of influence by the psychic is inevitable unless the psychic is extremely careful and responsible.

What happens when the psychic, in giving a reading misinterprets whatever he or she thinks is being said by whatever Being, Intelligence or 'Spirit' they think they are hearing on the other side, the other psychic side? What if in their egotistic, arrogant zeal to be right, they miss something, or do not truly know the situation?

Take the case of the psychic who predicted the

success of something her client had unsuccessfully tried previously. In this reading, the psychic predicted that her client would be successful the next time he tried it, and she was right: her client successfully killed himself that night. The psychic had a conscience and was horrified by what happened and never did another reading again. But this begs the question: why was the psychic unable to see or feel the man's emotional pain, his depression? The answer is because no psychic, no matter how seemingly 'gifted' or skilled will ever see 100% of anyone's future. People have multiple futures, dependent upon decisions made every moment of every day. And psychics only ever see _one_ *of those potential futures, at the moment, the client is in front of them.* This is why fortune telling is dangerous.

Psychics incur karma with every reading they give because undoubtedly, they do influence people in their lives. The argument can be made that the client *asked* for this help and that this absolved the psychic. However, when you seek to influence people, you incur karma in the process. Some intuitives are aware of this and accept this responsibility. However, some psychics with perhaps an inflated ego, do not fully comprehend the significance of their 'readings.'

Conversely, if you embark on a positive spiritual journey, study well and seek to help others, positive karma can be created. A good psychic will use their ability to enable the client to see for himself or herself

Tina Erwin

what is in the client's future by focusing on that person's own inherent healing abilities. A psychic schooled in spiritual law, will offer their client tools for self-discovery, but will never, ever abrogate their client's free will or make predictions - *ever*.

People have been begging psychics for centuries to tell them what their futures will be because some people want someone else to take responsibility for that future and they willingly give up their own free will to get those answers. But even this incurs karma because you are *never* released from your responsibilities or the future you create. Telling someone what their future is, does not absolve the recipient of the reading of the karma they create no matter what path they choose.

Karma is created when the psychic engages in telling the future and karma is created by the client for asking for the reading of the future. Consider simply for a moment why no psychic doing readings is wealthy.

Why are psychics routinely unable to win the lottery?

Psychics don't win the lottery, because psychics don't have the karma to see that future for themselves or anyone else.

Why are psychics routinely unable to predict when someone close to them will die or even their own death? *They cannot see this because no psychic has the karma for this knowledge unless there is a unique karmic circumstance.*

Why are psychics routinely unable to accurately predict world events?

Because there are an infinite number of factors that go into any event and the potential for change is ever constant.

Karma is accrued because the psychic convinces their clients to believe that their 'reading' is the real thing when whatever the psychic sees is but one potential future out of thousands. The other element here is that the future is changing second by second. **No psychic can ever keep up with what would be a massive algorithm of karmic calculations to determine what will happen next.**

And finally, no psychic can ever know the karmic bank account or the path of another person.

NEAR DEATH EXPERIENCES (NDE)

Many people have had a near death experience or an NDE. This means that a person is pronounced dead, either at the scene of an accident, in an emergency room, on an operating table or other scenario. It means that the authorities, and/or medical personnel, believe that the person has died. But the person does not 'stay dead'. They eventually revive, baffling those around them.

One of the main elements of this experience is the "panoramic life review." Some souls felt the speed at which they were shown their life review. The events that may have taken 40 years to live through flew by in mere seconds. They saw and felt the feelings of grief and pain they may have caused in others. Then the person felt that same grief and pain. The soul felt judged – at first. Later the soul realized that he or she was not being judged but was being given an opportunity to experience what others had experienced because of this person's actions. The soul realized that he or she was still loved. Then the soul was shown all the positive, warm loving actions they had done and how those were received. Karma offered the soul the opportunity to see and experience it all, in that one flash of light and feeling. And there was more.

Sometimes the person saw amazing spiritual beings. Some saw vats of fire and devils. Karma offered them an inside peak at the karma that they had created in the life just lived. Then, miraculously they were returned to mortal life, and they breathed again. Once afforded this deeper insight, they can now more thoughtfully choose how they will create their karmic path.

This NDE, is the moment as their life was ending, when they were able to see how what they did influenced the lives of others. Their firsthand preview showed how every action created karma and how this karma played out. Some souls were shocked and astonished by the beneficial as well as the detrimental effects that their actions created. This insight makes clear the unshakable nature of our responsibility for our thoughts, actions, words, and deeds.

WAR AND NEGOTIATION: THE PRICE OF VENGEANCE

If there are disputes between people, then negotiations must begin to resolve them for the mutual benefit of all peoples. If war develops then this breakdown represents a failure on both sides. If you win the war and destroy your opponent afterward then this karma will also come back to you. World Wars I and II are examples of this. The Allies after World War I and II are examples of this. The Allies after World War I were determined to punish Germany for initiating the Great War, the War to end all Wars. And punish them they did, to such an extent that they sowed the very seeds of World War II by their vicious hatred of this country and its people. This is why after World War II the Allies immediately began the Marshall Plan to rebuild Germany so that this country could become a powerful ally of all countries of Europe. They also rebuilt Japan. This enlightened approach precluded a third rise of violence in Germany and Japan against their neighbors. The irony here was that a compassionate approach did not stop the Cold War with Communist Nations. However, even that icy war was won without global casualties. Commerce trumped the machines of war – finally. It is fascinating to watch how the karma of Europe and the United States will evolve as countries focus more on economics than conquest.

Each of us has a very powerful ability to assist in

keeping war from happening by the power of prayer. Every prayer said, facilitates peace. Far from feeling helpless about world events, we can each play an active part in creating a peaceful world by the very act of sending healing energy - through prayer - to areas of trouble. Prayers must not demand that any person or country change to fit the view of the person sending the prayer. That is grey/black prayer, which means that it violates another person's or country's free will. By not asking anything in return, you create the most positive karma possible. Sharing your energy without judgment or expectation of reward is the highest form of giving.

KARMA AND THE EARTH

We each incur karma with the way we treat the earth and the resources that come from the earth. The genetic mutation of seeds is already dramatically damaging the fields, the birds, bees, other insects, and other plants near where these murder seeds are planted. Imagine the karma incurred when you deliberately, greedily plant seeds that kill any insect eating the plant. What does that same energy of death do to a human being when they eat those same plant products? Consider additionally that genetically engineering seeds that grow plants that produce seeds that cannot be harvested and used for the next season is creating horrendous karma for the companies who want to patent life in all its forms.

Companies that genetically engineer salmon to compete and potentially eradicate native fish populations again, earn terrible karma for themselves and all who are connected to them.

Look at countries that use fine mesh nets to capture all that is in the sea without regard to the damage this does to fish stocks, marine mammals, turtles, and other marine life forms. Now, this particular country is being inundated by gigantic jellyfish, which are clogging ports and coastal fishing areas. You reap what you sow.

Now consider the karma being created by countries seeking to harness the power of the sun through solar power, thereby reducing the dependence on fossil fuels. There is finally an appreciation for the finite resources of the earth. Consider that 12,000 homes 'go solar' every single month in San Diego County alone. Imagine the resource savings in this simple statistic.

Consider how blessed young Boyan Slat will be as he seeks to collect the staggering amount of plastic in the oceans of the world. This young man from Holland has invented an elegantly simple way to clean up the world's oceans. His service to the entire planet will come back to him karmically for lifetimes to come.

You probably have never heard of his name, but Yossi Leshem created and restored Israel's Hula Valley as a critical stopover for birds on migration routes. He worked to restore wetlands; he worked with farmers to use barn owls to rid fields of vermin instead of pesticides. He also works with the Palestinian Wildlife Society to track storks and griffon vultures Jordan is following his example in how to manage birds. Imagine that: Jews and Arabs working together to help nature. Imagine the karma for all of them working in peace to help nature and the world.

We could all be depressed about what is happening in the world, or we can choose to be inspired by progressive karmic deeds of so many unsung heroes of today and tomorrow. Karma has not collapsed on earth because so many people are working so conscientiously to save the world. Bless them all.

GOOD LUCK, BAD LUCK

There is a wonderful movie about a reporter who goes to Pennsylvania to report on whether or not the groundhog will see his shadow. In this movie, the reporter is unkind, sarcastic, belittling and feels as if the whole world is not only against him but that he is above the rest of the society. A snowstorm forces him to spend the night with his film crew in this tiny town. But while he is there, an odd thing happens: he finds himself in a time warp, re-living the same day again and again. Each day is the same as the last. He experienced multiple lifetimes in one – ever repeating - day. The only thing that changes is *how he reacts to that day*. He gets to know the people in the town; he learns to be of service to these people. He ceases his snobbish attitude; he joins them in the innocent dramas of their lives, and *he begins to contribute to making each of their lives a little bit better each day*. No one notices that each day is the same as the last; only our intrepid reporter realizes that he is stuck in karmic time and space do loop.

Each day our reporter slowly but surely improves as literally, months pass. He becomes beloved in the town and the woman he has been secretly in love with for quite some time, his producer, begins to fall for him, the *'new him.'* Although she remembers the 'old him' she finally learns to trust this new person he has become. He discovers that he loves doing service and he begins to revel in the warmth of the love that now showers him. Instead of spending his life feeling like he was on the outside looking into the windows of other people's lives, he has stepped inside the warmth of their embrace and felt their welcome. The movie ends with him being loved and revered by the entire town and best of all his producer falls madly in love with him. The finale of the film shows him finally awakening to a totally new day, with her by his side.

Was this a man with good luck or bad luck? Neither. The magic of the movies showed him his karma and forced him to face it, learn from it and change *himself*. He could not change anyone else. He could only change himself and when he did that, *everyone around him changed their attitude toward him*. His 'fortunes' dramatically improved on every level. He went from 'bad luck' to 'good luck' in one elegantly inspired movie.

The moral of the story is that karma will face you with the same lessons repeatedly until you learn the karmic/spiritual lesson, *so pay attention!* Once this has been learned, then you move on to the next level of your spiritual path, whether you know it is a spiritual path or not.

THE POSSIBLE DREAM: CREATING GOOD KARMA

How do you create good karma? Such a simple question and truly the answer is equally simple: *be the person you would like to respect, would like to love and care about.*

Maybe you had a terrible childhood, then work to make the world a better place for children. Carefully analyze what you learned from your childhood.

Perhaps your marriage did not work out. Study what you can from that marriage and divorce experience: learn from that powerful and heartbreaking period in your life. Why did you attract this person? Do you continue to attract the same type of person? How do you want your future companion to be different? How different will you be?

Are your children a disappointment to you? What did you do as a parent that contributed to their disappointing you? Could you have done things differently? We each reap what we sow, especially as parents. Did you keep your word? Were you a teacher? Were you there for them? What could you have done better, differently? What can you do within yourself to change, to be that better person?

Despise your boss? What is his or her terrible leadership teaching you? What critical lesson can you take from this person?

We are each karmically responsible for our bodies, what we put into our bodies, how we treat and/or mistreat our bodies. The karma of health and wellness is a direct result of how we chose to handle the lessons of childhood and how that lesson affects our bodies and souls as well as what we did or did not do to enhance our bodies as we lived our lives.

We are each here for service. What have you done to make the world a better place? Sometimes, it is simply to fulfill your role as a son or daughter, sibling, friend, parent, co-worker, boss, or even perfect stranger – to the best of your ability. All right, what if you have not been the person you would like to be? It is never too late to become that person. **There is no learning in perfection.** Learning from the past is truly why we are here. If you stopped doing the same thing over and over, took 'the higher road,' and vowed from this moment on to *be that better person,* then that is what intention you would set. That is what karmic statement you would make and that is how you begin to mitigate past karma and build a new karmic path.

We are each here to learn from the good, the bad, the tragic and the joyful moments in our lives. The point is to learn. The more we each learn, heal, hope, and help, the more we will bring to ourselves and those around us increasingly happier moments. Like Ebenezer Scrooge, looking at our past can enable us to welcome a brighter, happier, and more generous future.

Some karmic lessons are simply hard won. Make every lesson count.

KARMA IN THE SIMPLEST WORDS

Karma is always efficient.

Karma never wastes energy.

Karma is usually very clear.

Karma is eternal.

Who and what we have been dictates our lives in this moment. When we change who we are in this moment to being a different, more service-oriented person, then we instantly change our future. No one controls that but us. Karma gives us that control.

The more we each can find it in our hearts to love one another, the more love will there be in the world.

The easier it is to see the good in another person, the better reaction that person will have to us.

Be respectful of the earth, of nature, of those around you.

Release fear and suspicion. Be as wise as you can be which means that you think carefully before you speak, seeking only the most thoughtful words.

Karma cares not whether you attend any church, temple or structure of wood and stone to profess your love for God. Karma only cares about your *actions toward others* as you live each day. Live your faith, your belief in the goodness of others. Perform service in even small ways, and you will truly become God-like. It is in this way that karma will be served, and you will make mighty strides on your karmic path. But first, you have to raise your personal frequency.

Karma and Frequency

PART II

WHAT IS FREQUENCY OR VIBRATION?

You take the wrong exit.

You are excited to meet some friends for lunch at this new restaurant. You think you know the way, but somehow you take the wrong exit. The next thing you know, you are heading down a road that you have never been on before and in a part of town that you have never been to before. You feel very uncomfortable, and a subtle sense of fear is growing ominously within you.

This area of town makes you feel strangely vulnerable, so you lock your car doors and start looking for an exit out of this area quickly. There is graffiti everywhere, broken down cars and abandoned homes, trash, overgrown yards, and fields. It feels dirty and grimy, and you can't get out fast enough. The 'vibes' here are creeping you out. You don't want to be here. You are not sure why. Your senses are heightened and right now, you sense danger. You want to be back in an area where you feel comfortable, safe, and secure. This is pretty obvious.

But let's look at something that is less overt. What if you are in an area that is clean and kept up or you are in a gorgeous park or home and yet, you find that you can't wait to leave? *Something is making you feel uncomfortable that you can sense but cannot see.* Something in that area is lowering the frequency of that location and you can feel it.

What's happening to you? You are feeling the low vibrations of a negative location. This is frequency at its most basic level. But it is even more than this. **Frequency** can also be called **vibration** or **resonance**.

Did you ever hear a friend comment that they have just met someone and that they really connected - that they were on the same wavelength?

Did you ever notice that when you and someone else were not at all communicating, you felt that they were on a different frequency and that this is why you could not hear each other?

Have you ever noticed that, sometimes when you are with someone and you just feel like you are not communicating, that they cannot 'hear' you, and you are having a hard time 'hearing' them, that your frustration soars? What you are experiencing is a difference in frequency, a resonance difference so strong that you cannot communicate or connect with each other.

These are all elements of the concept that we each have a frequency, a vibration that we emanate, rather like psychic radar: active and passive radar. With active radar, we are looking for someone with our same resonant frequency because we would feel more comfortable being with them and being in certain locations. With passive radar, we just observe where we find that we are comfortable and with whom.

So, our own resonance, frequency or vibration is what defines us. This concept of frequency also influences our health and that is why we need to care so much about keeping our frequency elevated.

Our health is determined to a large degree by the frequency we emanate. The lower our personal frequency is, the higher the probability of illness. The Higher our personal frequency is, the higher the probability of wellness. Most illness caused by germs, viruses, and fungi are far more attracted to the person with the lowest frequency than to a person with a high frequency.

How do you determine your frequency? Well, ask yourself how often you are ill, or depressed, or have an accident (yes, a lower frequency will make you more magnetic to accidents as well.) The higher you raise your frequency, the less illness you will experience. But resonance, frequency, or vibration, is even more than this.

Everything in the universe vibrates. This vibration defines the movement of energy. Everything that vibrates has a frequency, a magnetism: your emotions, your health, your mind (how and what you think). All your senses pick up vibrations every moment of every day and your mind interprets these vibrations, these frequencies.

In addition, vibration revolves around the understanding **of energy or chi.** All objects, things, people, and our planet are composed of energy. We can see energy in lightning flashes, in the flow of rivers and in the rays that shine down to earth from the sun.

The power of the life force in each of us is the rate of our vibration. We can see and feel an individual's specific vibration as the glow of a healthy, vibrant person. A low vibration person can have an aura of illness, depression, anger, and hopelessness about them. Even people who do not consider themselves psychic can see and feel this difference. This is why when we meet someone we immediately and involuntarily notice their rate of vibration by how that person looks to us and how we feel within ourselves as we encounter this person.

Energy, chi, or life force is what enables all things to

live, function, grow, and excel. A lack of energy causes things to fail, slow down, become dysfunctional, and ultimately, die. Inanimate objects like stone, water, crystals, and earth also have energy. In addition to the critical energetic sources of the air and the sun - this energy is vitally important. Without the energy from these objects or things, people, plants, and animals could not function. We know that stones, for example, have an energetic signature because we seek certain types of stones for the subtle energies that they share with us. Rubies, emeralds, and diamonds have been sought for centuries for the beauty they emanate and their energetic and financial value. Quartz crystal has such a powerful energy that we use it in every single computer system on earth because quartz can vibrate on such a variety of frequency levels because of their piezo-electric qualities.

The earth and the sun are the main sources of energy for all things. But energy also comes from the heavens in the form of chi, Prana, or life force. We all generally, take the energy from the Earth and Sun for granted, yet there is no life without either of them. But is all energy the same?

No, there are different kinds of energy that extend up and down the energetic spectrum. What differentiates the levels and quality of energy is the vibratory rate or frequency by which each type of energy vibrates or moves. This then becomes the rate of vibration or frequency.

Homes all have a vibratory rate based on a myriad of factors. If a house is clean and uncluttered, has a well-kept yard and all are happy inside, this house will have a much higher vibration or frequency. But, if a house has an unkempt yard, a cluttered, filthy interior, that will be a house of a lower frequency. Hoarders are another example. If you are a person used to a neat and clean house, you will find yourself uncomfortable in the messy, dirty home of a hoarder. The opposite can also be true, if you are at home in a messy house, an uncluttered home will be uncomfortable for you.

All objects/things/people on the earth have a rate of vibration, and this rate of vibration is not static, it can be raised and lowered based on certain specific aspects in your life.

The rate of vibration has suddenly become a hot topic because the rate of vibration of the planet is rising. Most people will not be aware of this, but there is evidence to support this in what seem to be rising levels of insanity. As the rate rises, those who are not moving forward, trying to be a better person may feel growing levels of discomfort.

Mother Earth is considered by some to be a Spiritual Being (Spiritual Beings do not always take physical human form). There is a theory that as she grows spiritually, her *rate of vibration rises*. In the past, as her frequency slowly rose over centuries, people did not notice it. That has now changed. The frequency of the Earth is rising at an accelerated rate because the Earth is also evolving and as she evolves, her vibratory rate rises. As long as we are each working on raising our rate of vibration, we can keep up and enjoy better health, more meaningful relationships, and more advances on all levels. However, not everyone is aware of this rise and the need to continue to improve our individual frequencies. The disparity between those working to improve their frequency and those who are not, will, in some way, affect life on this planet. Therefore, we may want to do all we can to individually keep ourselves in as positive and healthy a place as we possibly can.

There is another aspect of chi/vibration. Chi, life force, Prana, and energy come from the cycle of life: the sun nourishes the earth, plants grow, animals thrive, rivers, and oceans team with positive life-giving energy.

However, the depletion of the ozone layer, the reduction of the quantity of rain forests through deforestation, the burning of fossil fuels, the pollution and depletion of life in the oceans, and the creation of vast amounts of air and electro-magnetic radiation pollution, make it harder and harder for us to acquire this positive energy, this essential life force.

WHY IS IT IMPORTANT TO RAISE YOUR FREQUENCY?

People who do nothing to raise their vibration may find their lives increasingly beginning to unravel - the spiritual bill is due. The more work you do to raise your vibration, the further along you find yourself on the spiritual path and the healthier and happier you will be. Look around you, there are growing levels of insanity as evidenced daily by the number of people who take the lives of others, children killing parents and other children, parents killing children, completely random acts of violence, road rage, the growing levels of cancers and other diseases, suicides, and the growing poverty consciousness and endless wars. This does not have to be; these alarming trends can be changed.

WHAT HAPPENS WHEN YOUR FREQUENCY IS LOW?

When your vibration is low, your resistance and immune system is low, which means that you are more susceptible to disease, unmanageable stress, accidents, colds, flu, and depression, your auric field is open to assault on many levels and your overall vulnerability to negative people, places and things increases. You may also have a heightened sense of victimization. Such a downhill spiral seems difficult to reverse. Keep in mind, that there are many variations on this theme, many levels of negativity, from despondent homeless people and severely depressed wealthy people, to people who have a high incidence of just bad days and one too many colds. People who feel that something is missing in their lives, or they are just not happy can reverse those negative feelings when they start to raise their vibration.

WHAT CAUSES A LOWER FREQUENCY?

Vibration is the key to successful, happy healthy living. In addition to environmental conditions, certain people, places, and things – which each of us have a surprising amount of control over - directly influence those feelings and ways of living. We can improve our environmental surroundings more than we realize. We all have freedom of choice. Some people consciously and subconsciously choose negative people, places, and things. This is not a criticism. For some people, it is all they have ever known. The negative aspects to avoid are:

A. People We all have bad days from time to time and may complain, become angry or fearful. After all, we're only human. For most of us, these emotions are temporary and are not a part of our core being. However, for other people, these traits can become a

Tina Erwin

prominent part of their personalities. Start looking around at the people who surround you. Begin asking yourself, "When I'm around Joe, do I feel energized or drained?" Become aware of people who consistently exemplify the following characteristics and do your best to mitigate those interactions.

Aggressive	Fearful
Angry	Gossip
Bigots	Self-Hating people
Bullies	Immature
Can't be pleased	Impatient
Chronic victim	Insensitive
Chronically ill	Lazy
Chronically Critical	Loner
Complainers	Jealous
Controlling	Impatient
Creates dramas	Immature
Critical of others	Manipulative
Cruel	Martyr
Cruel to animals	Narcissistic
Depressed	Nosy
Dishonest	Overly dramatic
Does not listen	Overly sensitive
Easily enraged	Passive aggressive
Egotistical	Petty
Energy vampire	Rage filled

Self-absorbed   Uncaring
Self-centered   Weak
Suspicious   Screaming/yelling

B. Places

Avoid spaces like these for extended periods of time, unless absolutely necessary. Living near these places causes a feeling of unease due to the **chaotic energy** resident there and/or the pollution they generate.

Airports   Haunted areas
Polluted water   Highways
Bars   Hospitals
Butchers   Landfills
Casinos   Low ceilings
Churches   Microwave towers
Cluttered areas   Night clubs
Crowded areas   Nursing homes
Dark spaces   Noisy places
Dirty places   Parking lots
Electrical substations   Power lines
Fight clubs   Power plants
Firing ranges   Prisons
Funeral homes   Schools
Ghettos   Smoking areas
Golf courses   Subways
Graveyards   Traffic centers

Treatment plants
C. Things
Avoid the following things, if possible, because so much of it carries **old auric residue**. Other things and life elements such as avoiding **always** wearing dark colors because this directly affects your view of life.

Alcohol	Fast food
Antique items	Fatty foods
Antique jewelry	News programs and
Broken things	papers
Constantly wearing	No scheduled eating
dark clothes	Noisy areas
Drugs (all)	Radiation
Dust	Rap music
Environmental	Sugary foods
pollutants	Tobacco

Used anything, where possible. Repurpose taking care to clean objects, bless them and make sure you know where they have come from and if possible, who owned them.

D. Spiritual Aspect
The following questionable spiritual aspects or practices are especially dangerous because you are tapping into the 'other side' without understanding the

full ramifications of that action. You may be inviting in whatever Being is possibly there. You may literally open a door to a very dark realm.

This same admonition applies to all those doing runes, channeling, table tipping, tarot, psychic readings, and violent video games. These practices tap into the other side without any idea of who or what is influencing you. You have no way to turn off their influence because it does not end when you put the game away or you think you have finished for the evening. You can receive horribly negative interference or harassment for years to come. Many times, the negative influence quickly affects your life, or it may affect it insidiously - slowly permeating all aspects of your life until the problems become almost insurmountable. Since these elements cause your vibrational level to be low, you can be more easily controlled and manipulated by those Beings who come through these video games.

Channeling is a favorite tool for those wishing to tap into the other side. Specifically, channeling is sitting in a roomful of people and mistakenly believing that you and/or your medium are being 'taken over' and hearing the actual voice of someone like St. Germain or Jesus. You have no idea who is really there. That voice you supposedly hear can be an extremely dark Being. Great caution is warranted here.

The Tortured cross (the one with Christ hanging in his

dying position on the cross,) has long been the black magician's tool. This concept may upset many readers, but it is important to understand the corruption of the beauty of the concept of the cross. The perpetuation of the visible torture of the beloved Master Jesus Christ is an extremely negative symbol and should never be used. It defiles and corrupts the power and high spiritual symbolism of the cross itself. The cross itself is fine and of high vibration.

Be mindful to remove these objects/elements from your life.

Angel Cards
Channeling
Chain letters/emails
Cults
Dabbling in black arts
Ghost hunting
Masks
Negative aspects of voodoo
Nazi items
Ouija boards
Revenge
Runes
Playing with ghosts
Readings
SéancesSelf-destructive acts
Self-destructive thoughts
Self-destruction words
Sending negative thoughts
Spell Casting tools
Table tipping
Tapping into the other side
Tarot cards
Tortured Christ cross
Violent video games

WHAT HAPPENS WHEN YOU DO RAISE YOUR FREQUENCY?

Many people can raise their vibration by simply doing some very common-sense things. These individuals may have no idea that this puts them on a spiritual path - it just seems like the right thing to do; that is great - all positive efforts help. The focus is the intent to have things improve so that your life is filled with the joy and abundance of health and love. Therefore, when you start doing little things like treating yourself to flowers once a week and breathing in that gloriously high vibration, you raise your own vibration a certain degree. Imagine if you were to take as many of the suggestions listed below and incorporate them into your life, how positive things could become. You would truly learn what it means to be in the harmony of the moment.

The list of things below constitutes a layered

approach. You don't just wear shoes. You wear layers of clothing to protect and preserve your energy. You would never walk or work outside naked in 20° weather. Your body would use all of its energy just keeping you warm. Well, when you have a low vibration, your body is doing the same thing - just surviving, not maintaining the physical body. When you wear numerous layers of loving, warm, protective, colorful clothing, you feel that you could work outside in the cold for long periods of time because you have protected and managed your body energy.

So, raising vibration is like adding layers of clothing to preserve energy on an icy day. If you do this, what might you notice? You just aren't sick as often, you find yourself surrounded by loving, positive people, your surroundings become more ordered and pleasant, you enjoy your job a bit more, you are not as impatient at little things, and you have more energy! You may also notice that some negative people are just not part of your life anymore. You may or may not miss them, but you will see this type of change. You have more insight and you just physically, emotionally, and spiritually feel better-you have more control over your life, and you see a more positive future.

Does this sound too good to be true: Why not try it and see how you feel over time. You may find you have more compassion for all those around you and you can view them without specific judgments. Judging people takes energy, energy that is not necessary to expend, energy that depletes you because most judgments are negative. Learn to view people and events in a detached way, without personal involvement unless it is necessary, and then only with compassion, but not intense emotion. You will find peace in this practice.

EMOTIONAL BAGGAGE KEEPS YOUR VIBRATION LOW

We all have an electrical system in our bodies, called our Charka system. Charka is a Sanskrit word for wheel. These energetic wheels are throughout our body. They help us to maintain our immune system.

In the study of the Chakra system, one of the aspects of keeping all chakras open, balanced, and functioning properly is the aspect of removing excess emotional traumas as well. In reality, it is these traumas, hurts and angers that keep our vibration low.

Revenge, rage, anger, and depression will lower vibration faster than almost anything known.

Someone once said that there are two basic emotions, love, and fear. When you are in love with life, all the cells in your body are filled with light and hope. You are able to work tirelessly because that light and hope carry you through stress, challenges, and difficulties. However, when somehow you are filled with the darkness of depression, that energy of fear, sadness, grief, rage, hopelessness begins to fill your cells and may begin to break down the entire body structure. Every action engenders a resonant reaction within the body and the more darkness you feel emotionally, the more darkness will fill your body. This may manifest in anything from simple headaches to full blown cancer. It is wise to remember that cancer is not contagious; it can be generated from within us by our own thoughts and actions.

Rape, incest, severe abuse, and deep grief all have the potential power to cause great internal harm to our bodies. Yet, the indomitable will and courage of the human spirit has the innate capacity to overcome all of these and not merely survive, but thrive, and make the world a better place and make a difference.

WHAT CAN YOU DO TO RAISE YOUR VIBRATION?

The suggestions listed below are a sampling of ideas you can use to raise your own vibration and change your resonance to a more positive frequency.

Some are costly, but others are common sense and require only modest effort. One of the most powerful tools is simply treating yourself to fresh flowers on a weekly basis. This small, wonderful habit will not only raise your own vibration, but the vibration of the people and physical area that surrounds you. Flowers are magic wands that process negativity - that is one reason why the water gets cloudy and must be changed - you are positively processing negative energy and transforming it into positive energy at a higher vibration. You are also reminding yourself of your own personal beauty and self-worth.

A. People

The characteristics you will want to be around will be people with the following characteristics.

At peace with themselves	Hopeful
Creative	Humble
Compassionate	Humorous
Constructive builders	Intuitive
Energetic	Kind
Find wonder in each day	Knowledge seekers
Fun	Loving
Gentle	Non-critical
Happy	Non-smoking
Have your best interests in mind	Nurturing
Healthy	Offer unconditional love
	Open to new things
	Patient

| Positive | Sense of humor |
| Responsible | Service oriented |

B. Places

Sometimes you need to get away and be in a place that has a higher frequency than your office or home.

Beaches	Lakes
Beautiful places	Light filled
Clean areas	homes/offices
Deserts	Oceans/seas
Feng Shuied	Places with beautiful
environments	music
Forests	Plants
Gardens	Ponds
Good smelling places	Trees
Inspirational places	Waterfalls

C. Things

"Things" go a long way in raising vibration. Sometimes when you can't get away from people or places, use "Things" to raise vibration, especially at your office on your desk. Some of these items clean the air of air pollution and put negative ions in the atmosphere, providing more natural life force. Other items are great for desks and offices to raise vibration.

Angel pictures/statues
Animals
Animal totems
Aquariums
Aromatherapy essential oils
Art (positive, uplifting images)
Beautiful things
Bells
Blue lights inside
Buddhist malas
Color
Crystals
Electromagnetic Protectors
Bathe with Epsom Salts
Essential oils
Feng shui cures

Fountains
Fresh flowers
Full spectrum light
Green lights at night
Herbs
Incense
Ionizers
Liquid minerals
Mirrors
Music
Noni juice
Organic fruits & vegetables
Radionic devices
Rainbow makers
Plants
Pure water
Purple/violet objects
Salt lamps
Sunlight
Vitamins

D. Spiritual Aspects

There are wonderful tools you can use to raise your frequency. Some are physical and some are spiritual. All will help you to improve your spiritual frequency. Some of these tools, like salt, clean your auric field.

Tina Erwin

Gratitude
Open-mindedness
Be with positive
people
Cleanliness
Create wealth feeling
Crossing over prayer
Exercise
Feel you deserve
happiness
Instrumental chants
Learn to love yourself
Learn about spiritual
 world
Meditation practices
Neatness
Own mind/body
connection
Quiet (find places to
enjoy quiet peace)
Practice compassion
daily

Pray
Protective practices
Remove old emotions
Remove ghosts
Read/study
Say mantras
Watch metaphors and
signs
Yoga/qigong
Service
Spiritual white light
Stress analysis
Understand karma
Wash hands
Watch dreams
Watch "emotional
 buttons"
Watch life symbols
Watch metaphors and
signs
Yoga/qigong

APPLYING THE RESONANCE CONCEPT

Now that we understand that resonance/vibration/frequency is/are an aspect of how much harmony we have in our lives, let us learn how to apply this element of harmonics.

What keeps us in harmony? Did you ever notice that some people just seem to attract trouble? No matter what happens, these souls would find themselves literally magnetic to trouble. Then there are the people who are in harmony with legal problems. Attorney fees are just a part of their monthly budget. It is their norm.

What causes us to be in harmony with something - to be in resonance with a situation be it violent, legal, sickness, wealth, or success?

Let us look at sickness. Have you noticed that there

just seem to be an unnatural number of people with cancer? For example, breast cancer. There is not a day that goes by that some periodical is not publishing something about breast cancer. It is literally on every magazine you pick up. There are awareness days, get yourself checked days, visit your doctor days, racing marathons and now they even have people wearing wrist bands and jewelry for breast cancer. We are putting half the population in resonance with breast cancer and (surprise!) women are getting breast cancer in staggering numbers. Ever notice that no one comes up with a cure for this or any cancer despite billions being donated, people getting checked and bless them, people running themselves literally to death to beat cancer and finding themselves running right into it?

So, stop the music! Hold the harmonics in abeyance! Take a hard look at what norm you want to have to define you. What choices are you making? Here is an example of how it works:

If you are chronically angry at this horrible unfair world, then you will seek every venue to right injustice - hence you are just going to spend a lot of time with lawyers and the court system.

Terrified of getting cancer? Well, then you may be asking for the experience of what you fear the most. Stop being so afraid and decide to *be well*. Take off that toxic pink wristband and send healing to the whole world and be in resonance with prayer not cancer.

Do you find angry people and drivers wherever you go? Do you find that you just may be an angry driver? Decide to change your resonance - try this frame of mind and say to yourself: *everywhere I go and everywhere I drive I meet the nicest people, the friendliest people and have the best experiences.*

Are you in resonance with poverty consciousness - the frame of mind that there is never enough money? Did you grow up hearing your parents say that there is never any money? Well, they pretty much convinced you that there would also never BE any money in the future, so you will never be wealthy. That frame of mind, that poverty consciousness resonance is a choice. Choose to change it. New frame of mind: there is always a wonderful supply of money. I am such a wealthy person, money can and does fall out of the sky.

What about folks who are loners – who say they never have friends as if it were someone else's fault that they are alone. To have friends you have to *be* a friend. Be in resonance with friendship. Look in the mirror and decide if you would be friends with you and if you don't like the answer, then change the only person you have any control over: yourself. Be a friend.

If all your friends are irritable angry people - then you may find that you are irritable and angry as well. Find happy friends. Decide to *be* happy and happy friends will be in resonance with you.

Resonance/harmony/vibration are such intangibles and yet they can completely define our life. We create karma with every breath we take. Some people are afraid of that karma, of living. Some people just rush out and embrace it and love living with tremendous exuberance and others just survive each day. How we resonate, what we vibrate with and with whom, help define our karmic path. Stop your world for just a microsecond, analyze it and then decide if you need to change that with which you are in resonance.

How Can You Possibly Make All These Changes?

Well, you probably cannot do them all at once, but you can begin. It is easiest to begin with flowers and plants. Some of the other items are costly and you can budget for them over time. You can also begin to evaluate your attitude toward life and begin to view things, situations, even traffic tie-ups differently. These lists are designed to give you options and create an awareness so you can start at your own pace. Did you recognize some negative personal habits or practices here? One of the key elements of healing your subconscious is understanding the elements of your old emotional patterns. Until you do this, and face your own personal demons, you cannot truly raise your vibration to the level you would desire. Invest in yourself. You are worth it. It is worth the time, money, and effort to seek these personal changes. Do you need help changing them? When the student is ready, the teacher will be there. This is true; decide to change your life this moment. If you need help changing old patterns, look around, you may just find that the right teacher appears.

WHY FENG SHUI IS CRITICAL IN RAISING FREQUENCY

When you decide to improve your vibration, you set your intention. Setting intention is the first step in manifestation. The reason Feng Shui works so well is that it forces you to focus intention on every area of your life in a balanced way, to see the energy flow in all areas of your life as equally important. The person who is only interested in money forgets that family and relationships are critical to happiness and wonders why the money did not bring happiness.

Balance is a key element in raising vibration: you can feel the difference. Feng Shui teaches you how to balance your environment to bring peaceful wonderful energy to every area of your life and home. It puts you squarely responsible for your own happiness and empowers you to make it happen. Your home is your sacred space. But as you became more intuitive, you begin to notice how you feel wherever you are.

Whether you consider yourself 'sensitive' or not, a remarkable number of people can readily feel when a place feels terrible. You walk in and your skin crawls, or the 'flight or fight' feeling comes over you and you can't explain it. Sometimes a room just feels 'off,' and you find yourself avoiding that room or space.

However, when a room is balanced on every level, you find yourself enjoying being there. Happy moments are there, and life feels more peaceful and nourishing. It is important to allow yourself to *be sensitive* to your surroundings; begin to notice what feels wonderful and why and what feels icky and why. This is the essence of Feng Shui: feeling where you are and seeking to understand the balance or lack of balance wherever you are.

THE VITALITY OF THE BODY ELECTRIC

We are beings animated by an electrical system within the body. The flow of electricity is the flow of chi or energy in the body. Any blockages in this flow will create problems in the vitality of the body and stop the energy that is vital to a healthy life.

Sleep is critical for the human body. During the sleep times, the body does all its repair work, rebalances chi and restores the cells. This process balances all the electrical functions in the body and keeps chi flowing smoothly. Without sleep, eventually the person's body breaks down. One of the key elements to keeping chi flowing in your body is to have plenty of deep, nourishing sleep. This directly affects all mental processes.

If you feel out of balance, have problems sleeping and feel that your vibration is dropping – and the more sensitive you are, the more you will be able to feel this – then try acupuncture. This 5,000-year-old ancient Chinese medicine process brings a person's body back into balance, restores correct energetic flow and facilitates sleep. This restorative technique will dramatically slow aging, keep the body electric operating normally and raise vibration. Part of rebalancing this emotional flow is the requirement to address our level of depression. Clogged pathways make us feel down, sluggish, and mentally fogged.

The body electric is the life force that keeps our bodies animated. That animation represents all the electrical signals that course through our body telling our body to blink, swallow, sweat, sleep, dream, feel hunger, pain, love, despair. The volume of life force that flows through us is directly related to our sense of personal power. This sense is in direct correlation with our vibration. The higher your vibration, the more powerful will you feel the life-affirming Chi flow through you. This means that you are consciously rebalancing your own energy to keep it in that high frequency place.

But what happens if you become down, or suffer a tragedy? No one lives a life without experiencing these events at some point. Focus on renewal, retreat to a place that is emotionally and spiritually renewing/cleansing in nature. Waterfalls, oriental gardens, the desert, with its open timeless expanses may often lift you out of your sad emotional places.

Engage in heartfelt prayer. Go ahead and cry and allow the pent-up energy to be released. If you find that crying is difficult, watch a sad movie and allow yourself to identify with the on-screen characters and cry. Be kind to yourself and you will be restored.

THE VIBRATION OF MUSIC AND COLOR

Have you ever been in a store/restaurant and lingered there because the music was so wonderful, it relaxed you? This isn't just good marketing; it is healing as well. Have you ever been in a store/restaurant and just could not stand to be there anymore because the music was so awful, loud, and vicious? The vibration of music can be healing, soothing, inspiring, or destructive, chaotic, or depressing. It is the actual vibration of the individual tones that affects us. When a particular tone hits a specific charka directly, we can really feel it. There are actual tones/notes for particular chakras, which can directly affect our moods and actions. Beautiful music raises vibration. It is the specific harmonics of music ranging from Mozart and Chopin to our modern-day composers such as John Williams or Jerry Goldsmith, which cause our spirits to soar. Fill your home/car/office with high vibrational classical music. Many businesses/police know that playing classical music in high crime areas such as in malls, stores, places where people loiter, is a deterrent to criminals. Why? The vibration of a criminal is low, and the vibration of the music is high therefore the music conflicts with the low energy of the criminals, which actually makes them uncomfortable...too bad! Wonder what would happen if they played classical music in prisons?

Surrounding yourself with beautiful colors, clear tones in your room, clothing, and decorations will inspire your soul and cause you to feel healthier. Drab, dark colors create a sense of fear, hopelessness, and depression. Notice the colors in an Oriental Garden.

Cool greens, blues, light grays with color accents create a feeling of calm serenity. People think of these places when they want to meditate - because the colors allow you to go within yourself, in peace.

FEAR DRAMATICALLY LOWERS VIBRATION

Fear seems to be all around us, penetrating everything we see and feel. We don't want to be afraid, but we are. It owns us. If love is the ultimate reality, the final goal, then we must all come face to face with that primal fear and convert it to love, even when it is the hardest for us.

Why does fear lower vibration? Because it causes "un-ease" which eventually leads to "dis-ease." When you can't conquer your fear, it owns you and eats away at all you think you have built. But until you can conquer your own fear, truly own it, you live a hollow life.

Is it possible that there are only two base emotions: love and fear, as Neal Donald Walsh notes in his *Conversations with God* series of books? If this is true, then we must be extremely mindful of how we face those elements in our lives that often yank us back to that place of almost primal fear. News shows, violent TV dramas, brutal video games and angry talk among people, fosters the festering of fetid fear that will poison our minds and bodies. We must resist these elements and move forward with love in our hearts.

Anger is a natural part of living, but it does not have to rule our hearts. Prayer helps to remove fear and reconnects us to the Divine. Consistent connection to the Divine, and feelings of gratitude for the positive elements of our lives, will bring us back to a place of love.

As we each advance spiritually, we begin to find that there is a growing level of love for all people of the earth: people we don't know, people who may even wish us harm.

Fear will never engender healing, only love will do that. The more we can love with all our hearts, the stronger we will become.

One of the Universal Spiritual Laws states: "that which you fear the most - you draw to you." This is magnetism: things, and energies being drawn to you. God offers terrific incentive to learn the lesson. In so doing, you end up freeing yourself from the horrible burden of fear and therefore raising your vibration in the process. Remember, the vibration of fear is physically, emotionally, and spiritually destructive.

Tina Erwin

RAISING VIBRATION IS A LIFELONG COMMITMENT

The aspect of raising your own personal vibration can be daunting. There seems to be so much to do. Raising vibration is not so much a series of acts as it is the beginning of a spiritual journey. You never leave this journey. Hence the things you do to raise vibration, you do forever. This means that you do spiritual practice and prayer daily. You care for your body daily. You constantly add a new vibration-raising tool to your repertoire. If you bring in a Feng Shui practitioner to help you balance your surroundings, you follow through with the cures; you spend the money to create the balance. Then you never stop Feng Shuing your life. You are always sensitive to clutter, dirt, broken things, or things that don't work.

Tina Erwin

You always seek balance.

The aspect of raising your own personal vibration can be daunting. There seems to be so much to do. Raising vibration is not so much a series of acts as it is the beginning of a spiritual journey. You never leave this journey. Hence the things you do to raise vibration, you do forever. This means that you do spiritual practice and prayer daily. You care for your body daily. You constantly add a new vibration-raising tool to your repertoire. If you bring in a Feng Shui practitioner to help you balance your surroundings, you follow through with the cures; you spend the money to create the balance. Then you never, ever stop Feng Shuing your life. You are always sensitive to clutter, dirt, broken things, or things that don't work. You always seek balance.

You evaluate all people in your life and this includes in-laws who act like outlaws, friends who are energy vampires, jobs that you hate and people who victimize you. You decide if you will keep these people in your life.

Never stop raising vibration. It is a lifelong mission until you take your last breath.

Raising vibration is the clearest most direct path to becoming a Lightworker, to doing service for yourself, your family, and the world. As you increase your vibration, your family, children too, will benefit from

102

this shift. They will learn how to raise vibration and how good it feels and perhaps learn to pay it forward by teaching others how to increase vibration. It means you take your place among Spiritual Beings by understanding the Universal Force, the God force, that life is precious and that since you have it, you must make it matter.

RAISING YOUR SPIRITUAL VIBRATION

What exactly does this mean? When a person lives and breathes anxiety, fears loss of control, feels envy, anger, hate, depression, illness, and constant fatigue then this person will inevitably draw situations to them that will have these negative energies. In addition, if they gossip, they lower their vibration; they lower themselves spiritually. They symbolically dig a big, dark hole and crawl in it. They complain to anyone who will listen about how hard their life is, what a mess things are and how many people are against them. Is this perspective of their lives true? Do they really hate it? Does misery love company? Are they surrounded by other negative people; do they live in negative soup?

Whatever perspective a person has is their truth. Only that person can decide if he or she wishes to change that truth. Your wanting them to change does little good. Leaving books, hints, articles about being more positive is not going to change them. There must be a trigger that they recognize as the signal that they do not have to live like this anymore. They choose. That person must ask for help in the immediacy of the moment. They must believe that they are worthy of help, growth, and change. That person must be able to see for themselves the difference between people who are happy and healthy (notice how these two words always seem to go together?), and those who are miserable. When you are this emotionally low, it takes quite a bit of courage to pick yourself up and change. It is frankly like bending steel, but even steel bends under the right circumstances.

If you know a person as described above, notice how much better you feel when you are not with them, lighter somehow, less oppressed. A low vibration is exhausting. When you are with happy people, people of high vibration, you feel energized when you are in their presence. They do not "weigh" you down with their issues, they are interested in how you are, the state of the world and how to help and are always finding and learning something new - creating new neural networks in their own brains. These people challenge you to see the world in a better way – and yourself along with it. These are people who have done their share of spiritual work and see with compassion and caring how hard you are working toward your own vibrational growth.

Change your thoughts. Adopt a different perspective. Make this new view your waking thought and those thoughts will be love, hope, abundance, and joy. Fear must have victims to have power. When you deny fear its food, it dies. Control your thoughts and you can empower your entire life.

WHAT WOULD HAPPEN IF EVERYONE RAISED THEIR OWN VIBRATION?

There would eventually be no war or "dis-ease." Violence would begin to cease and as people became at peace with themselves, world calm would seep into the consciousness of all people. The planet would begin to heal because we could more closely feel the Earth's vibration and the need to send loving kindness to all living things and inanimate objects as well as people. We would be less likely to create ugliness in our thoughts, deeds, art, music, food, writings, environment, and intentions. Compassion would rule the day. Hopefully that is coming. We all have a role, let us be sure to play our most positive part.

Actually, that is the plan: for the world to raise its collective vibration. Many people are just not there yet, but a few are leading the way. If each of us took a moment and sought to remember our ultimate Divine connection, looked for that spark of Heaven in ourselves and others, we would feel it – even for a moment – we would be lifted up a bit each day.

Souls lost in the sea of despair, depression, confusion, and loneliness have forgotten that they are each a child of a loving God. The experiences we are offered allow us the freedom to make better choices each day. Perhaps at some point these souls will begin to lift their faces up to the light and remember who they are, who they may have been and what they can ultimately become.

Once this process begins, then the soul begins to see and feel the hand of God in everything around them. The miracle of life is the miracle of God, the Divine, and it lives within each of us and all of nature.

WHAT ABOUT FUTURE LIVES - IS THERE A DNA CONNECTION?

One of the amazing benefits of raising your vibration is the concept of restoring your DNA. It has often been thought that DNA is static, that it cannot change and that you are "stuck with what you have" forever. That is now believed to be untrue. The more you work to change your environment, improve your body and your overall health, cleanse the body of toxins, the more you can restore your DNA to its original level. Original as when the earth was new, and disease and centuries of patterns had not become imprinted on your DNA.

You can also extend your lifetime by having DNA that just works well, by having a body that is in harmony with itself and people and the environment around it. Your sense of peace and happiness are extended. The concept of original sin is replaced with a concept of peace, love, and happiness for all your life.

The belief is that the condition of the body you leave this life with is the body you can start out with in the next life. Mitigating factors include, of course karma and the life lessons each soul chooses to learn which may include illness. Hence, the more gratitude you show for your wonderful body, the better care you take of it, the better body you will return with next time. Heal your life today and enjoy a potentially much more wonderful future life.

YOUR PERSONAL MISSION

For each of you who reads this information on Vibration and comes away with an understanding of what you can do to raise your vibration and how you can do it, there is this added benefit. Everything you do not only helps you, but also everyone with whom you come in contact. You will grow and as you do so, you will be touching many other lives. It is the miraculous process of becoming a Lightworker. The higher you raise your vibration through the use of every tool you can find, the more service you find yourself doing, the more you help the world and the more you advance on your own personal path of enlightenment. Attract abundance and happiness through your higher frequency, higher vibration. It is through this process that you truly learn the meaning of living and teaching only love.

ABOUT THE AUTHOR

Tina Erwin CDR USN (Ret) has studied metaphysics all of her life, gaining insight into the interpersonal relationships at the heart of everyday living. Her writing comes from an intense desire to know and understand the unseen world of action and reaction, combined with a sincere desire to share this understanding with other knowledge seekers. Her first book, The *Lightworker's Guide to Healing Grief,* is a treatise on how to help yourself or someone else to heal grief. Her second book, *The Lightworker's Guide to Everyday Karma,* is a lighthearted look at applying the principles of karmic law to everyday life.

Her third, fourth and fifth books, *Ghost* **Stories** *from the Ghost's Point of View Trilogy, Volumes 1, 2 and 3,* introduce what it is like to be dead, what it is like to discover that the life you thought you were going to have is never going to happen. Literally you see the ghosts' point of view.

Soul Evolution, Past Lives and Karmic Ties offers a down to earth in how we progress and build on our karmic paths.

The Crossing Over Prayer Book, 88 Extraordinary Prayers to Help the living and the dead is a concise and critical tool for anyone with a genuine desire to help the living and the dead.

Her lifelong studies into the deeper meaning of events and actions were further enhanced by the experiences of a dynamic, 20-year career in the Navy, working for the U.S. Submarine Force, retiring at the Commander level. Commander Erwin found the Navy to be a tremendous schoolhouse in which to study all the facets of behavior, from the worst to the finest levels of humanity.

Tina has been happily married to the love of her life, submariner, CDR Troy Erwin, USN (Ret), for 50 years.

She has produced an extensive collection of videos, which can be found both on YouTube and on her websites: www.TinaErwin.com. www.GhostHelpers.com

You can learn more about her books, podcasts, and her videos on her website: www.TinaErwin.com or connect with her: Tina@TinaErwin.com. Please also check out www.GhostHelpers.com and you can also contact her through: Contact@Ghosthelpers.com.

Be sure to listen to her podcast on the GhostHelpers app and on Amazon.com.

www.ingramcontent.com/pod-product-compliance
Lightning Source LLC
Chambersburg PA
CBHW061959040426

42447CB00010B/1817